AI SKILLS

A Short Guide to Staying Relevant in the Age of Artificial Intelligence

MANOJ KUMAR NAIR

notionpress.com

INDIA • SINGAPORE • MALAYSIA

CONTENTS

Contents

INTRODUCTION

Artificial Intelligence is changing the way people study, work, and build careers. Yet most students and IT professionals feel confused about what AI actually means for them. Some fear job loss, while others feel pressure to learn everything about AI without knowing where to start. This book exists to remove that confusion and replace it with clarity.

AI is not about becoming a data scientist or learning complex algorithms. It is about understanding how to work alongside intelligent tools that are already shaping daily tasks, decisions, and productivity. When used correctly, AI becomes a powerful assistant that improves learning, communication, and problem-solving. When misunderstood, it becomes a source of anxiety and poor decisions.

This book focuses on practical AI skills that matter in the real world. It is written in simple language and designed for students, freshers, and working IT professionals who want to stay relevant, confident, and future-ready in the AI era.

Artificial Intelligence is reshaping how work is done across industries.

This book focuses on practical AI usage for students and IT professionals.

The goal is clarity, not hype; application, not fear.

Chapter 1

AI REALITY CHECK - WHAT IS ACTUALLY CHANGING

Artificial Intelligence is changing how work is done, not who does the work. The most common misunderstanding is that AI replaces people. In reality, it replaces inefficient processes, repetitive mental effort, and slow workflows. This distinction shifts the discussion from job loss to productivity and skill evolution. AI feels disruptive because it now assists with writing, analysis, and decision support—tasks traditionally considered human.

AI does not think, understand meaning, or take responsibility. It identifies patterns in data and predicts likely outcomes. This makes AI effective for structured tasks but unreliable for decisions requiring judgment, ethics, or accountability. Treating AI as intelligence rather than a tool leads to misuse.

From a career perspective, the real risk is not AI adoption but resistance to change. Those who adapt workflows gain clarity and efficiency, while those who resist gradually lose relevance.

Chapter 2

HOW AI REALLY WORKS

To use AI effectively, you do not need to understand algorithms or advanced mathematics. What matters is understanding how AI behaves. AI learns patterns from large datasets and generates responses based on probability rather than understanding intent or meaning.

This explains why AI can sound confident while still being incorrect. Output quality depends on data quality, clarity of instructions, and context. When prompts are vague or incomplete, results become unreliable. Human review is therefore essential in academic and professional use.

Students and professionals should treat AI as an assistant, not an authority. Understanding how AI works helps prevent overdependence and encourages responsible, effective usage.

Chapter 3

WHERE AI IS ALREADY USED TODAY

AI is not a future technology—it is already embedded in daily life. People interact with AI through search engines, recommendation systems, spam filters, navigation apps, and digital assistants. These systems analyse patterns continuously to improve outcomes.

In education, AI personalises learning platforms, recommends study material, detects plagiarism, and analyses performance. In workplaces, AI supports monitoring, log analysis, ticket routing, and performance optimization.

Understanding where AI is already used reduces fear and confusion. Awareness allows students and professionals to adapt faster and make better decisions about how to use AI productively.

Chapter 4

THINKING WITH AI

The most important AI skill is not technical expertise but the ability to think with AI. AI performs best when humans provide direction, context, and judgment. It should support analysis and idea structuring rather than replace thinking.

Poor AI usage involves blind copying and unquestioned acceptance of output. Effective usage involves asking clear questions, refining responses, and applying critical thinking. The quality of results depends on how AI is used.

For students, thinking with AI improves understanding. For professionals, it improves productivity and decision quality. AI amplifies human thinking rather than replacing it.

Chapter 5

PROMPTING AS A PROFESSIONAL SKILL

Prompting is how humans communicate intent to AI. As AI becomes common in work and study, prompting has become a critical digital skill. Poor prompts lead to generic or incorrect responses, while clear prompts produce useful results.

Effective prompts include context, constraints, and expected output format. Prompting is an iterative process that improves through refinement and follow-up questions.

For students, prompting helps explain concepts and prepare answers. For professionals, it improves documentation, communication, and analysis. Quality input directly determines quality output.

Chapter 6

AI TOOL LITERACY – CHOOSING WHAT MATTERS

Thousands of AI tools are available today, but using too many reduces effectiveness. Tool overload creates confusion and shallow understanding. Productivity improves when a few reliable tools are mastered deeply.

AI tools fall into categories such as writing, coding, design, analytics, and automation. Selection should be based on reliability, ease of use, integration, and data privacy.

Tool literacy means knowing what a tool can and cannot do. Mastery comes from repeated use and thoughtful application, not constant experimentation.

Chapter 7

USING AI AS A STUDENT

For students, AI should be a learning assistant, not a shortcut. Used correctly, it explains complex topics, provides examples, and structures study material to improve understanding.

AI can help with revision planning, practice questions, projects, and presentations. However, students must ensure they understand content rather than submit AI-generated answers blindly.

Misuse weakens learning and becomes visible during exams and interviews. Responsible use builds confidence, clarity, and long-term capability.

Chapter 8

USING AI AS AN IT PROFESSIONAL

In professional environments, AI acts as a productivity multiplier. IT professionals use AI to draft emails, prepare reports, write documentation, and summarise complex information. These capabilities reduce routine effort and free time for higher-value tasks.

AI is also widely used in technical work such as code generation, debugging support, and learning new technologies. While AI can accelerate execution, professionals remain fully responsible for accuracy, security, and outcomes. AI suggestions must always be reviewed before implementation.

For managers and team leads, AI helps with communication, planning, and data summarisation. Professionals who use AI responsibly gain efficiency and clarity. Those who ignore it risk falling behind as expectations continue to evolve.

Chapter 9

AI FOR COMMUNICATION AND VISIBILITY

Clear communication has become a critical career skill, especially in technical roles. AI helps students and professionals express ideas more clearly by improving structure, tone, and readability. Emails, reports, and explanations can be drafted faster and refined with less effort, reducing common communication gaps.

AI is particularly useful for documentation. It can convert rough notes into structured documents, standardise formats, and improve clarity. Good documentation reduces dependency on individuals and improves knowledge sharing within teams. This increases both efficiency and professional credibility.

AI also supports professional visibility through resume refinement and content preparation. Visibility is not self-promotion; it is the ability to communicate value clearly. Professionals who use AI to articulate their work accurately are more likely to be recognised and trusted.

Chapter 10

AI IN SOFTWARE DEVELOPMENT

AI is changing how software is developed, but it does not replace the need for strong fundamentals. Developers use AI to generate boilerplate code, understand unfamiliar codebases, and identify errors more quickly. This accelerates development and reduces repetitive effort.

However, AI-generated code is not always correct or secure. Developers must review logic, handle edge cases, and ensure security standards are met. Overreliance on AI without validation leads to fragile systems and technical debt.

The most valuable developers treat AI as a junior assistant rather than a senior architect. AI helps with execution, while humans handle design, judgment, and accountability. Strong fundamentals combined with AI support result in higher-quality software.

Chapter 11

AI IN CLOUD, DEVOPS, AND INFRASTRUCTURE

Infrastructure roles are evolving as AI enables systems to become more predictive. In cloud environments, AI is used for anomaly detection, capacity planning, cost optimisation, and performance monitoring. These capabilities improve system reliability and reduce operational stress.

In DevOps, AI assists with log analysis, pipeline optimisation, incident prediction, and faster root cause analysis. This shifts teams from reactive firefighting to proactive operations. Problems can be identified earlier, reducing downtime and impact.

Despite automation, human oversight remains essential. AI can suggest actions, but professionals must approve and execute decisions. Infrastructure stability depends on judgment, context, and accountability, not automation alone.

Chapter 12

AI IN DATA, ANALYTICS, AND DECISION SUPPORT

Data becomes valuable only when it leads to insight. AI helps analyse large datasets, identify patterns, and predict trends more efficiently than traditional methods. This improves the speed and quality of decision-making across organisations.

AI-driven analytics allows even non-technical professionals to ask better questions and understand data-driven insights. Instead of complex reports, AI can summarise trends and highlight risks or opportunities in simpler terms.

However, AI should support decisions, not replace them. Context, ethics, and business understanding remain critical. Professionals who combine AI insights with human judgment make better, more responsible decisions.

Chapter 13

AI IN CYBERSECURITY AND IT RISK

Cybersecurity is one of the earliest domains where AI changed both attack and defence strategies. Attackers use AI to automate phishing, generate convincing messages, and identify vulnerabilities at scale. This increases the speed and sophistication of cyber threats, making traditional manual detection methods less effective.

Security teams also use AI to analyze logs, detect unusual behavior, and prioritize incidents. AI helps reduce alert overload by highlighting patterns that require immediate attention. This allows teams to focus on real risks rather than reacting to every signal.

Despite advanced tools, cybersecurity decisions cannot be automated completely. AI can identify anomalies, but humans must assess intent, impact, and response. Careers in cybersecurity continue to grow, especially for professionals who combine technical skills with judgment and responsibility.

Chapter 14

HOW AI IS CHANGING IT ROLES

AI is not eliminating IT roles; it is changing how responsibilities are distributed within them. Tasks that are repetitive or rule-based are increasingly automated, allowing professionals to focus on analysis, decision-making, and improvement. This shift changes job expectations rather than job titles.

Roles such as manual testing, basic support, and routine reporting are evolving. These roles now require skills in automation oversight, exception handling, and interpretation of results. Professionals who adapt their skill sets remain relevant and valuable.

Roles at risk are those that involve repetitive execution without learning or ownership. Career stability comes from developing skills that involve judgment, coordination, and problem-solving. AI accelerates change, but learning determines outcomes.

Chapter 15

AI SKILLS RECRUITERS ACTUALLY EVALUATE

Most recruiters are not looking for AI specialists or data scientists. They are looking for professionals who understand how AI improves their work. The ability to explain practical AI usage is more valuable than theoretical knowledge.

Recruiters evaluate candidates based on problem-solving ability, communication clarity, and adaptability. Candidates who can demonstrate responsible AI usage with real examples stand out. Buzzwords and certifications without application are easily identified and often ignored.

During interviews, candidates are increasingly asked how they use AI in daily work. Honest explanations build trust. Recruiters value awareness of AI's limitations as much as its benefits. Practical understanding is the strongest signal of readiness.

Chapter 16

USING AI FOR RESUME, INTERVIEWS, AND CAREER GROWTH

AI is a powerful tool for improving how professionals present their experience. It helps refine resumes, structure achievements, and align content with job descriptions. This improves clarity but does not replace real experience.

For interviews, AI supports preparation by generating practice questions and helping structure answers. It can highlight gaps in explanations and suggest clearer ways to communicate experience. Confidence comes from preparation, not automation.

Long-term career growth depends on continuous learning and reflection. Professionals who use AI to review skills, identify gaps, and plan development stay competitive. AI supports growth, but responsibility for progress remains personal.

Career growth depends on continuous learning and reflection, supported—but not replaced—by AI.

Chapter 17

A STRUCTURED AI LEARNING ROADMAP

Many people fail to learn AI effectively because they approach it without structure. Random videos, tools, and courses create confusion rather than progress. A structured roadmap helps learners move steadily without burnout or frustration.

The first phase should focus on foundations. This includes:

Understanding how AI works

Learning basic prompting skills

Using AI for small daily tasks.

The goal is familiarity, not mastery. Regular use builds confidence and removes fear.

The second phase involves applying AI to real studies or work.

Learners should integrate AI into assignments, projects, or professional tasks and measure productivity gains.

The final phase focuses on long-term integration, where AI becomes part of regular workflows.

Consistency matters more than speed. Small, steady progress produces lasting results. Consistency matters more than speed for long-term results.

Chapter 18

ETHICS, RISKS, AND RESPONSIBLE AI USAGE

As AI becomes more powerful, responsible usage becomes essential. Misuse of AI can lead to data breaches, biased outcomes, and loss of trust. These risks affect not only organisations but also individual careers.

One major risk is sharing confidential or sensitive information with AI tools. Another is blindly trusting AI output without verification. AI can produce confident but incorrect responses, which can lead to poor decisions if not reviewed carefully.

Responsible AI usage requires clear boundaries. AI should be treated as an assistant, not an authority. Users must verify outputs, follow organisational policies, and remain accountable for decisions. Ethical behaviour builds credibility and trust, which are critical assets in long-term careers.

Chapter 19

STAYING RELEVANT FOR THE NEXT DECADE

Technology will continue to evolve, and AI is only one part of that change. The most important skill for long-term career success is the ability to learn continuously. Tools will change, but adaptability remains valuable.

Professionals who stay relevant actively review their skills, remain curious, and respond calmly to change. They focus on understanding fundamentals rather than chasing every new trend. This mindset reduces anxiety and increases resilience.

Careers are not built on single technologies but on habits of learning, reflection, and improvement.

AI rewards those who adapt thoughtfully and consistently. The future belongs to individuals who grow with change rather than resist it.

Chapter 20

AI SKILLS TO LEARN IN 2026

As AI becomes part of every industry, success in 2026 and beyond will depend on skills, not job titles. Students and IT professionals don't need to master everything. They need the right mix of understanding, application, and mindset. Below are the most important AI skill categories, along with tools or courses to learn them and the benefits they offer.

1. **AI Literacy & Conceptual Understanding (FOUNDATION SKILL)**

What to learn:

How AI works at a high level, its limits, risks, and ethical use.

Courses / Learning Options:

AI fundamentals courses (non-technical)

Introductory AI explainers and case-based learning

Benefits:

Removes fear and confusion

Helps you talk about AI confidently

Builds strong decision-making ability

This is mandatory for all students and professionals, regardless of role.

2. **Prompting & AI Communication Skills**

What to learn:

How to ask AI the right questions and refine responses.

Tools to practice:

AI chat assistants

AI writing and planning tools

Benefits:

Better answers with less effort

Saves time in studies and office work

Improves clarity and productivity

This skill turns AI from a toy into a serious assistant.

3. **Data & Analytical Thinking (NOT Data Science)**

What to learn:

Understanding data quality, patterns, trends, and basic interpretation.

Courses / Tools:

Data literacy courses

Spreadsheet tools with AI features

Business analytics dashboards

Benefits:

Better decisions

Reduced dependency on others

Strong advantage in corporate roles

AI runs on data—understanding data multiplies your value.

4. AI Productivity & Automation Skills

What to learn:

Using AI to automate routine tasks and improve efficiency.

Tools:

AI-based email, document, and meeting assistants

Task automation and workflow tools

Benefits:

Saves hours every week

Improves work quality

Reduces burnout

This skill is a career accelerator.

5. **Domain + AI Skill Combination**

What to learn:

Applying AI in your own field—IT, HR, finance, operations, or education.

Courses / Learning:

Industry-specific AI use cases

AI for business / IT leadership programs

Benefits:

Makes you irreplaceable

Opens leadership and transition roles

Future-proofs your career

AI rewards those who combine experience with technology.

6. **AI Ethics, Risk & Governance Awareness**

What to learn:

Bias, privacy, security, and responsible AI use.

Learning options:

Ethics and governance modules

Corporate compliance training

Benefits:

Protects reputation and career

Builds leadership credibility

Essential for managers and IT leaders

Final Advice

You don't need to become an AI expert. You need to become AI-capable, AI-aware, and AI-confident.

Learn steadily, apply wisely, and grow continuously. That is the real AI skill for 2026 and beyond.

CONCLUSION

Artificial Intelligence will continue to evolve, but the principles that shape successful careers remain the same. AI is a tool that enhances productivity, learning, and decision-making when used with clarity and responsibility. It does not replace human judgment, creativity, or accountability. Those strengths remain essential and irreplaceable.

Throughout this book, the focus has been on practical understanding rather than hype. You have seen how AI fits into studies, IT roles, communication, and long-term career planning. The goal is not to use every AI tool available, but to use the right tools thoughtfully and consistently. Small improvements in how you work with AI can create significant long-term advantages.

The future belongs to individuals who remain curious, adaptable, and willing to learn. By using AI as a support system rather than a replacement, you can stay relevant, confident, and in control of your career—today and well beyond 2026.

ABOUT THE AUTHOR

Manoj Kumar Nair is a seasoned Information Technology professional with over twenty-five years of experience driving technology transformation across manufacturing and R&D focused organizations. Today, he heads Information Technology for a multinational organization.

Manoj's career spans successes and setbacks, major technology shifts and industry disruptions. From long nights during go-lives, audits, and cyber incidents to leading digital transformations, he has lived the full evolution from "doing IT" to "leading IT."

His writing focuses on simplifying complex technology concepts and presenting them in a way that everyday readers can understand and apply in real life. His work includes the popular books like

Digital Arrest, AI Explained Simply, and ChatGPT & Generative AI.

www.ingramcontent.com/pod-product-compliance
Lightning Source LLC
LaVergne TN
LVHW090432210926
848480LV00002B/797